Poets of Bulgaria

Edited by William Meredith

POETS OF BULGARIA

Edited by William Meredith

Translated by. . .   John Balaban
Roland Flint
Richard Harteis
Josephine Jacobsen
Maxine Kumin
Denise Levertov
William Meredith
May Swenson
John Updike
Theodore Weiss
Daniel Weissbort
Reed Whittemore
Richard Wilbur

FOREST BOOKS

London 1988

Published by Forest Books
20 Forest View, Chingford, London E4 7AY

First published in the United States of America 1985
by Unicorn Press, Inc.
First published in the United Kingdom 1988

Typeset in Great Britain by Cover to Cover, Cambridge
Printed in Great Britain by A. Wheaton & Co Ltd, Exeter

Jacket design © Ann Evans
Original work © Bulgarian Poets c/o JUSAUTOR, Sofia 1986
Introduction © Alan Brownjohn

British Library Cataloguing in Publication Data:

1. Bulgarian Poetry — 20th century —
Translations into English

2. English
Poetry — Translations from Bulgarian
I. Meredith, William
891.8–113–08   PG1145.E3

ISBN. 0–948259–39–6

Translations have more than aesthetic value. They can be culturally and politically valuable too. Throughout history, cultures like ours have reached moments when they need other perspectives, like mirrors, in which to examine themselves. The advantage can work both ways even if the translation is going only in one direction. As Meredith once replied to a Bulgarian journalist: 'the wide, general interest in translation in our time is surely a manifestation of a wide, general concern for understanding between cultures.'

John Balaban
The Pennsylvania State University

CONTENTS

ACKNOWLEDGEMENTS

Some of these translations have been published in *The American Poetry Review, The New England Review* and *Breadloaf Quarterly, Ms., Mundus Artium, The New Orleans Review* and *The Poetry Miscellany*. These and 'Two masks unearthed in Bulgaria' from William Meredith's *The Cheer* are reprinted by permission of Unicorn Press. Bozhidar Bozhilov's poems first appeared in *American Pages* (International Poetry Forum Byblos Edition V).

Forest Books wish to thank the Union of Bulgarian Writers, the Unicorn Press, and the following translators whose assistance made both these editions possible: Vassil Athanassov, Cornelia Bozhilova, Elena Hristova, Valentin Kostov, Aseneta Nick, Vladimir Phillipov, Alexander Shurbanov, and Alexandra Veleva.

INTRODUCTION

The topic of translation attracts quite a lot of not-very-useful attention from linguistic theorists who are not practitioners, and would not always be capable of a particularly sensitive response to the literature being translated.

Of course translation is a complicated art; but the issues are simpler than they are sometimes allowed to appear. Translation is an absorbing process; but there is something wrong if it does not feel, to the translator, laborious and ordinary for much of the time, as tough and unglamorous as most writing really is. One of the most distinguished translators of drama, Michael Meyer, has declared (and he exemplifies the principle admirably in his own book) that a translation should be a *window* through which the audience, or the reader, can see the original work; a surface retaining, as far as possible, no removable spots or flaws, and certainly showing no new blemishes put there by the egoism of the translator. This is duller, and more valuable, work than painting a new picture.

What happens in translation is often, and unfortunately, rather different, because a number of forgiveable temptations lie in the path of different kinds of translator. There is the temptation of academic formality: the academic translator, equipped with knowledge of the language and a zeal for absolute accuracy, will work with precision, but raw — perhaps unconsciously — on a tradition of dogged and stiff translation. He or she, whether translating a poet of the past or the present, will not necessarily have absorbed the tones and usages peculiar to poetry in our time (more likely absorbed those of the immediate past), and a crash course with half-a-dozen anthologies would not be enough. This is a disabling deficiency. It is essential to grasp some of the ways of modern poets, because a translation ought to speak to readers in our own time in the language to which they have become used.

Sadly, there cannot be a fixed and definitive academic translation of anything, because no linguistic register is going to be timeless, with the possible exception of the registers of those few geniuses — Shakespeare and Goethe among them — who have, so far, transcended time and compelled us to go understanding them on their own linguistic terms, if we are reading them in the original: they are great defenders of their languages. So there may be relatively timeless originals, but never a timeless translation. The greatest works should offer new encouragement to, and elicit new vigour from, new translators in — about what period? — perhaps every new half-century.

But the best efforts will not be academic translations. The academic translator's work may be an honourable product, indispensable for reference, as they say. There are meticulously exact, even robust or sensitive, academic translations from past poets or modern poets, which are useful and command respect. But their manner is not, and cannot be, the manner for today. Translations can date with mysterious ánd frustrating speed, and these are frequently dated even before they see the light of print.

The poet-translator, especially if engaged on the poems of a dead poet or a living poet he has not had the opportunity to meet, may be prone to another temptation: that of feeling too self-confident in the possession of the right, up-to-date poetic equipment for the task. He or she is not only a poet (and, one hopes, a good and respected one), and has access through his own practice and reading to the modes and techniques of verse in our time, but also someone used to wrestling with meanings, and delighted to receive flashes of inspiration when they come. Translation can be hard and bitter work; but suddenly, after hours of struggle armed with dictionaries, or thesauruses, or just with the resources of one's own diction (and the work of translation can be a most humbling reminder of its limits) magnificent solutions will suggest·themselves.

It is just such moments of apparent insight, the arrival of dazzlingly bright ideas, which must be mistrusted in translating poetry (though they may happen more often in translating drama, where a playwright-translator, or a director, will be tempted to invent opportunities for meaning or action which are not justified by the original, thus inserting radical misconceptions and changes into a text.) They are the places where the work can leave the rails altogether. The process of translation ought to consist of hard, level-headed and level-hearted, application to the responsibility of getting things as right as possible, and sounding as good as possible in the language to which they have been transferred. There should not be any importation of one's own irrelevant excitements: translation ought to be an effort of enthralled, but calmly controlled, dedication.

This excellent and widely varied selection of modern Bulgarian poetry is testimony to a profound dedication on the part of the editor and contributors to getting the method right. While he was Poetry Consultant to the Library of Congress, William Meredith paid several visits to other countries, and developed a particular fascination with the culture of Bulgaria. Somehow he persuaded a notable group of fellow American poets to share this enthusiasm with him, and embark on translations of poets whose work he had come to know and admire. The fervent interest of John Balaban, a poet who is fast becoming a translator extraordinary – from Romanian, Russian and Vietnamese as well as Bulgarian – gave the venture added impetus.

In his introduction to the American edition of *Poets of Bulgaria*, John Balaban writes:

... we were provided with some very accurate, word-for-word trans-literations of the Bulgarian poems. Some of us know Bulgarian or Russian. Talking with our Bulgarian translators, and often with the poets themselves, we listened to the originals and asked questions – questions about form and metre, about diction, about the power of an image – until we had a good idea of what the poem was doing in the original and what it might do in English.

This would have been slow, sure, detailed, difficult work, but work of exactly the right sort; not just the right method, but with living poets the *only* suitable method. The poetry of the Bulgarian poets deserved it, and the results are a tribute to the devotion, assiduousness and realism of their American poet-translators.

It is possible to read these translations and adaptations (the distinction is fairly made where appropriate) as if they were *not* translations, and yet gain a sense of fidelity to the originals. The reader recognises the influence of the traditional in the older writers — mixed with a defiant adventurousness in Elisaveta Bagriana — a discernible modernism in others, and a strong flavour of the different in all of them. The style, and the culture, seem refreshingly unfamiliar, and that is as it should be. Translation should not involve assimilation of a work to the assumptions of our own time or society, or for that matter the talent of the individual translator: the work translated should disconcert and challenge with its *difference*.

These Bulgarian poems should, and in these admirable translations they do, convey something new. Contact with this newness, with the courage and expansiveness, the lyrical freedom and the lurking alarm in the work of Luchesar Elenkov, Nikolai Hristozov, Boris Kristov and Lyubomir Levchev (to name only some), should be valuable and stimulating for English readers and poets, who are accustomed to powerful virtues of quite another kind in their own modern poetry. Forest Books are to be congratulated on taking over the torch lighted by the Unicorn Press in publishing the first, American edition of *Poets of Bulgaria*, and continuing a fruitful process of contact between cultures and poetries which will learn much by appreciating how different they are from one another, and how strikingly diverse.

Alan Brownjohn

TWO MASKS UNEARTHED IN BULGARIA

BY WILLIAM MEREDITH

When God was learning to draw the human face
I think he may have made a few like these
that now look up at us through museum glass
a few miles north of where they slept
for six thousand years, a necropolis near Varna.
With golden staves and ornaments around them
they lay among human bodies but had none.
Gods themselves, or soldiers lost abroad—
we don't know who they are.

The gold buttons which are their curious eyes,
the old clay which is their wrinkled skin,
seem to have been worked by the same free hand
that drew Adam for the Jews about that time.
It is moving, that the eyes are still questioning
and no sadder than they are, time being what it is—
as though they saw nothing tragic in the faces
looking down through glass into theirs.
Only clay and gold, they seem to say,
passing through one condition on its way to the next.

THE POEMS

THE POEMS

Elisaveta Bagriana

THE ELEMENTS

Who can keep the northwind that blows across the hilltops
from whistling through the passes, lifting clouds of chaff up,
ripping slates from house roofs, canvases from wagons,
toppling fences, gates, small children in the play parks
in my home town?

Who can hold the Bistritsa back from its spring torrents,
breaking up the ice jams, breaking struts and bridges,
spilling from its stream bed, mischievous and muddy,
into house and garden, flooding out the livestock,
in my home town?

Who can turn the wine back that's begun fermenting,
once it's in the casks set in walls that breathe out moisture,
on which in strict Cyrillic is printed *red* and *white,* in
those cold and stony cellars built by our forefathers
in my home town?

Tell me, who can stop me, free thinker and free wanderer,
blood sister to the northwind, to water and to wine,
lured beyond all boundaries, beckoned to by vastness,
I who dream of open roads, unseen, unmapped, untrodden;
who can stop me?

(M.K.)

Elisaveta Bagriana

AMAZON

Always the morning
cool on my face—
for I am young, young, young
with heart ablaze.

My lively horse
trots tireless and bold—
before my eyes
a seamless world unfolds.

Who follows the sparks
his horseshoes strike?
Behind me leaps up
a song of light:

We'll get to Helicon
just at sunrise—
fly, winged horse,
destiny is ours.

There under your hoof
light springs into air,
flows forth in a new stream—
lifegiving, pure.

And when my sisters
join us, the flame
of inspiration
will blaze up in them.

Over our hard-won
victory, the stars
of Perseus and Andromeda
will watchfully flicker.

(M.K.)

DESCENDANT

None of my ancestors sat for their portraits,
none of my kin kept a family album
and nothing's come down to me of their precepts,
their faces, their sayings, their lives, their feelings.

But I feel the old and impetuous
blood of the wanderer pulse in my veins.
It wakes me at night, a furious force,
driving me out to commit my first sin.

Maybe some dark-eyed grandmother's mother
dressed in a turban and silks of the harem
eloped in the night with her foreign lover,
ran off in the black with her noble darling.

Maybe a clatter of galloping horses
echoed across the Danubian plain.
Maybe the wind brushed away all traces
and saved them both from the dagger's pain.

This may explain why I go on loving
the breadth of the steppes too vast for the eye,
the dance of the whip, the horse's hard galloping
and snatches of voices the wind hurls to me.

Call me a sinner, beguiler, baiter,
maybe I'll break down midway on life's road.
Nevertheless, I'm yours, your own daughter
and you, my earth-mother, you are my own blood.

(M.K.)

Miriana Basheva

MONDAYS

We all slave
for the same big shot
the Calendar,
full of the old dog's hope
that by some chance
on Monday
we'll learn new tricks.
O.K! So that's it:
on Monday
I'll quit smoking.
I'll tidy up this house
and this head.
Simply said, "I'll push
right up front
with those looking
for this or that.
Let's go!
I'm leaving behind
all my neurotic ways.
You bet. That's it.
For years on end
it's always been a sort
of Tuesday. Next Monday
I'll be good as new.
I'll teach the calendar
patience, reverence, faith
in a Monday style.
Yet one thing's clear:
Should I marry on Sunday
on Monday, I'd be divorced.

(J.B.)

Georgi Belev

LIFE

I get more and more tangled in my fears,
I stagger from one day to the next,
a rooster tied by its feet, for sale—
my wife beside me is the same way.
We're nice to each other, accommodating.
Meanwhile our pink-colored daughter, the lie, is growing.
She behaves herself, doesn't shame us,
eats well, maybe too well.
She was born only a day or so ago,
yet has already reached puberty.
We worry at night, what with all the riffraff.
But she doesn't run around, keeps a lustful eye on me instead—
She spies on me in the shower.
I know what's going to happen!
I've even started making preparations—exercise, a diet.
I'm liberated, young but experienced.
A lie in love with a lie!
Is incest between lies a sin?
Our progeny is already springing up—more lies.
We are packing the house.
I step on bellies, legs, ears,
they never even cry out, they multiply
like amoebae, only quicker.
They swarm, drop off the ceiling
into my spoon. . . Ugh! Cannibalism!
My wife shuts her eyes and swallows.

But is it she? Her breathing's different
and her nostrils and upper lip
quiver, coming closer and closer. . .

I'll sleep apart, barricade the door
with my life: a life term.

Georgi Belev

"With our bed," the lie corrects me.
And then with her brawny sweaty arms
she pins me down in a final hold.

(D.W.)

Georgi Borisov

LET HIM BE

Let the man be who had nothing to tell you,
let him mumble his beard over his mug of gall,
let him work his bread into bits at the table.
Let him think he's coughing because the tobacco's damp.

And let him, as he leaves, nod goodbye to the bottle
and go outside and leap from the porch into the night
and stride across the fields already thick with clover
to wave down the first truck that finds him in its lights.

Let him tell the wicked driver all about his ulcer,
how it keeps him up, hungry at odd times,
and how bread is not enough, no, not by bread alone
despite whatever may be the common thought.

Let him get off at a hill and go up to a pear tree
and punch his fist right through the twisted trunk,
clean through to the night, and, as the tree listens,
let him curse it in pain and shame and bitter hurt.

Because, life picks us up like little chunks of ryebread
and wads and works us in its rough, sweaty fist.
So let him be, this man who's walking down the hillside.
Let him alone. Let him slam the table with his fist.

(J.B.)

Georgi Borisov

A TALE

And then, worn by the sun, I fell asleep
stretched on the grass beside a cricket's trill
where a busy spider waded in my hair
wavering out a brilliant web.

Ants peeped in my nostrils.
A locust fanned its wings upon my brow.
And finally my nose became an ant-hill
with many secret ways and windings.

A snug little lizard sunned on one palm.
A perky sparrow nestled in the other.
I felt the earth becoming soft and gentle
and deep in my dream the sky sank from above.

And then it rained. It rained through me
for three long days and nights. It stopped.
I listened. The earth rolled and rustled
as the grass rushed green through my eyes.

(*J.B.*)

Bozhidar Bozhilov

ODE TO NOISE

And what strength have we
to fight noise?

The sea roars all the time,
even when the wind dribbles.
In the forest, branches and leaves rustle.
Bees hum in dark swarms like stars.

But in hospitals and cemeteries
it's quiet.

My heart beats.
Outside my house
trams, buses, people rumble.

My noisy little girls
really enjoy talking, crying, laughing.
My wife says the same old things
and sings a hymn with the vacuum cleaner.

A hunk of bread hears the noise
my old mother makes
with a knife and fork and butter frying.
On my typewriter I tap an ode
to the sweet, incessant noise
of rhythm and rhymes which otherwise
would melt silently
into nothing.

(Cornelia Bozhilova)

MEN

Men stand alone by the river.

The water reflects the bridge and runs
down toward other men, also alone.

Who are these men
by the river, silent,
who stand all day
without the smile of a woman?

They are actors, poets, artists. . .
If there is a distracting dress nearby, it will impede
the flowing of their thoughts
along the granite pier.

If she came with a kiss, it would disturb them.
If she came to talk, it would disturb them.
If she loved them, it would disturb them.
If she despised them, it would disturb them.

They are silent and alone by the river,
alone with Paris.

(C.B.)

POETS
for Paul Engle

In a motor boat in dark water
Men undress silently.
They are no longer poets,
They are happy children.

The water circles their bodies
In a greedy embrace.
The night has never been so dangerous
Or friendly for any of them.

The black poet recalled water
With the drums of crocodiles.
He recalled the stars of hunger
In the dreams of his children.

The yellow poet recalled rain
Over the scorched black bay.
He recalled clearly the voice of death
In the organ pipes of gun barrels.

The white poet didn't recall a river.
For rivers are dry in his country.
He saw how the enemy fords
His country's free landscape.

And the poet born near this shore
Didn't recall anything because
Here he is always handsome and strong,
Thick-haired, smiling and tender.

(C.B.)

Bozhidar Bozhilov

RELATIVITY

A Chinese impression—
Overloaded junks come from the ocean,
Sunk to the deck in water.
They stop by the stone wharf.
Their crews come ashore.

A foreigner, musing, asks them
Whether they have sailed across the Black Sea.
The yellow sailors rebuff him.
They haven't even heard of a sea
With such a strange name
Anywhere in the world.

The foreigner then contemplates
His poems
And recalls his friends
Who are poets.

(C.B.)

Atanas Dalchev

44, AVENUE DE MAINE

What rotten luck has dumped me here
before this cramped-in court
so dwarfed it cuts a day in half
and cannot sprout a tree?

Above the nearby railway house
smoke hangs in heavy haze.
I stand before my window-sill
and stare out at the trains

which shunt on in and whistle out
on rails that sing like wires,
while I am closed in darkened rooms
along the rattling tracks.

(J.B.)

Atanas Dalchev

SNOW 1929

Upon the slanted iron eaves
and on the asphalt lanes
will pure snow rush down
like a radiant angel? Not likely.
Here in this city black as a coal,
winter comes smeared and foul
and frightful to snow and angels.
For if angelic snow should fall
the cop and the whore would tramp it
and feathery snow would be smirched
by mill and depot smoke.

Pure snow can only gather
in parks where children play.

(J.B.)

THE TREE

It was one of those gray blocks of flats, several stories high, with numerous small cement balconies and window frames with paint peeling off—it was one of those human beehives, simultaneously the outcome of the thirst for property and poverty. I saw this uninviting, cheerless façade at the end of the street every day. Almost daily I had occasion to pass it. My footsteps, which faded away while I was passing the block, suddenly sounded louder at the entrance. In spite of that I would never have known anything about its inhabitants had not a chance errand, which an acquaintance of mine from the country had asked me to perform, got me to cross its threshold.

I began climbing the stairs and stopped before I got on the landing before I got to the fourth floor. I looked down from the staircase window. I saw a desolate courtyard, surrounded by buildings and in the middle a large tree, in yellow autumn hues.

This solitary tree, whose existence I had never suspected behind the block, struck me. I stood at the window and watched the wind blow off a leaf or two from the branches; the leaves would fall on a balcony, or hit the wall and then fall straight to the ground.

Then suddenly I recalled having seen the same tree behind a wooden fence. It was tall and graceful, its branches spread out, and was a feast for eyes of the passers-by. Then the workmen began building the block of flats and suddenly it had disappeared.

Some people, suffering from incurable illness, are bedridden for years. At first their acquaintances wonder at not seeing them: then they no longer wonder, and forget about them. The tree had found itself cut off from the people and the world long ago, and now, alone in a gloomy narrow courtyard it was dying, forgotten by all.

(V.A.)

Atanas Dalchev

ON LEAVING

Well, why should I be sad to go?
I had no friend or lover here.
I walked about and tipped my hat
to winds that blew away the year.

(J.B.)

Blaga Dimitrova

THE ROAD
(Version 1)

When the road dips down,
into shadows and doubts,
it seems exitless.
When upwards it swerves
so steeply breath grows short
an expanse opens up.
But at the crest I am dazed
by the rhythm of farther ridges,
by the blue hypnosis
of ever new distances.

(J.U.)

THE ROAD
(Version 2, with echoes of Emily Dickinson)

When downward dips the roadway
In valleylike recess,
The shadows darken doubtfully,
Appearing exitless.

But when the road, relenting,
All upward swiftly flies,
Expansiveness too open
Confounds my eyes.

Retreating ridges' rhythm
Then mightily renews
The distances and distance's
Hypnotizing blues.

(J.U.)

TRAVELLING ALONE

Until I reach the future
countless roads must be traversed.
Will you be waiting for me still?
The wind and my hair are as one,
the sun beats red in my blood;
as soon as my arms wrap around you,
the whole hot country of me
will assimilate you.
But when will that day come?
Space and his partner time,
those relentless amortizers
of even the longest-lasting feelings,
will dwindle your love and betray me!
Yet, I have confidence
in the rigorous, exacting roads
and set out upon them alone.
At all points I am accompanied
by the tender, true, and majestic
dear profile of the Balkans.
It whispers to me on the roadway
with a voice I remember from childhood,
it whispers ancient tales
and legends freshly coined.
Solitude cannot be borne
away from home.
Only in my own land
can I be heroine enough
to travel always alone.

(J.U.)

PAIN

You are leaving.
The day musters its smile.
Beyond you, possibility closes down.

Suddenly into my breast
pounds a meteorite
and each breath becomes pain.

It burns so deep inside
flames curl up out of depths
mysterious though mine.

From these chasms I deduce
my possible, unattained summits.
Leave, then.

(J.U.)

Blaga Dimitrova

THE WATER BUFFALO
(HANOI, 1972)

The rain drizzled and shifted
over rippling green fields of rice.
Every drop will grow a grain.

The lop-eared banana leaves
opened an umbrella over me
and I sank into an ancient hush.

An old man with a buffalo
stood at the end of the path.
Both were carved in wood.

Without a word the old man
parted a curtain of leaves
to let me into his house.

I stepped across the threshold
and froze before a gaping hole,
a crater bigger than a grave.

Smoke rose from ashes,
black smoke curling in the wind.
Dry wells, instead of walls.

My host slid down to the bottom,
calling me, with beckoning hand,
to his family in the pit.

His grandson—a tuft of hair,
His old woman—the handle of a pot,
His strapping sons—bloody stones.

His pretty girls—threads of cloth,
His sons-in-law—sandal thongs,
His daughters-in-law—lumps of earth.

His brother, on a visit—a broken stool,
His great-grandson, still in the womb
of his mother—a banana shoot.

The shoot, as if still growing,
had a green bud which resembled
the clenched fist of a baby.

. . .To have lived a long life honestly,
to have raised a big family
by yourself, and in your old age

to be left alone with your buffalo,
the only living creature
with whom to share your sorrow.

The inventions of America, those
gadgets, machines, technical wonders—
is this what they are for?

(J.B.)

Blaga Dimitrova

CASSANDRA WITH A TAIL

A cat stretches from one end
of my childhood to the other.
Those winters, by the hearth,
it spun a yarn of smoke into a ball.
At night, it flickered half-moon eyes
in the dark corners of the house.
By day, its tail twirled a signature
on the sky. It pawed the air with grace,
gathering in its coat
the electricity of the storm
and smoothing it into glossy fur.
Wise. With cottony steps.

Self-possessed.
Just once she jumped out of her skin.
One peaceful evening
her tail shot up like a bottle brush
and she leapt onto the chandelier
wailing like an ambulance
as if all the voltage in her fur
exploded out in flashing rage.
None of us understood the cat's prophecy.
We hissed at her to calm her down. . .And
the earthquake nearly flattened the house.
The oracular cat disappeared,
with my childhood, forever.

Blaga Dimitrova

But her miracle stayed with me.
Tonight, to my surprise,
she crept inside me.
Bristling with shock, I shook
and bounded back from wall to wall
yammering up a piercing cry
to call you wherever you are:
Listen. You have so little time.
Grab what you can,
whatever is dear, whatever you love.
Deep in the belly of the earth
an atomic blast is swelling up,
nurtured by electronic brains,
and produced by pulsing robots.
This green careening planet
spins blindly in the dark
so close to annihilation.
Listen. *No one listens.* Meow.

(J.B.)

Blaga Dimitrova

WHO TAKES CARE
OF THE BLIND STORK?

Perched on a chimney upon one leg
as if impaled, it doesn't see
the weathervane below its bill;
doesn't mind the shuddering antennas
but stares over its beak like the key
to doors of distant chambers
where dawn crows to come out.
Don Quixote in feathery nightgown
ready to sweep his windmill wings.

Blind, it doesn't note at all
the dark campaigns of the clouds
nor the quarrels of the nearby marsh
but sits stuck on a bare chimney pot
unruffled in the acrid smoke.
Black as a chimney sweep,
our patient messenger of joy.
Nothing moves it but the wish
to snatch up the first streak of dawn
and bear it everywhere upon its bill.
The rosy infant. The old myth.

"Just one thing I can't make out,"
croaked a frog in the shadowy marsh,
"why the wind's scythe, the rain's flails
haven't yet shorn its wings."

(J.B.)

LULLABY FOR MY MOTHER

At night I make her bed
in the folds of old age.
Her skinny hand
pulls mine into the dark.

Before her dreams begin,
from a brain erased of speech,
a small cracked voice calls *mama*
and I become my mother's mother,

and am jolted
as if the earth's axis tilted
and the poles reversed.
Where am I?
I have no time for speculations.

Flustered, I wipe her dry
just as she once taught me.
Mama, she whispers
worried at being naughty.
A draft streams from the window.

Heating pad. Glass. The pills.
I tip the lampshade back.
Mama, don't leave me alone
all by myself in the dark.

She chokes her sobs
as I take her in my arms
so heavy with pain and fear.
She or me? In cold winter
a double cradle breaks.

Please wake me early.
I need an early start.
Is anything left to do?
Which of us left work undone?

Mama, my child, sleep.
"Little baby bunting. . ."

(*J.B.*)

Blaga Dimitrova

A WOMAN ALONE ON THE ROAD

It's a risk and a bother
in this world that's still male
when around each bend may lie
ambushes of absurd encounters
and the streets fix her
with cold stares.
This woman alone on the road.
Her only defense
is her defenselessness.

She hasn't made from any man
a crutch, or wayside shelter.
She never walked over a man
as if he were a bridge.
She went off alone
to meet him as an equal
and to love him truly.

Whether she'll go far
or falter in the mud
or be blinded by horizons
she doesn't know. She's stubborn.
Even if rebuked along the way
her setting out itself
is accomplishment enough.
A woman alone on the road.
And yet she goes on
and does not stop.

No man can be as lonesome
as a woman on her own.
Before her the darkness
drops down a locked door.
A woman alone on the road
ought not go out at night.
The dawn sun, like a turnkey,
will unlock her horizons.

Still she goes on
even in darkness
not glancing about in fear
but each step measuring her faith
in the Dark Man
with whom she's been threatened
for a long time.
Her steps echo on the paving
and stub against a stone.
A woman alone on the road:
quiet brave steps over a sad earth,
an earth which, against the stars,
is a woman alone on the road.

(J.B.)

Georgi Djagarov

BULGARIA

A land—a human palm
but I wouldn't want you bigger.
I'm glad your blood is southern blood
and your old sinews flint.

What if wolves and jackals used to howl
in your fields and forests?
You've been good to those who are good to you,
to foes you show no pity.

A land like a human palm,
yet it was this rough hand that broke
the chalice of Byzantine poison
and the curved sword of the Turk.

Traffickers in tobacco and blood
used to parcel out your land for sale.
You felled them with broken backs—
you're small but you're heavy.

And then a miracle occurred: death righting death.
The houses with wooden porches smiled,
great banners fluttered.
The way that opened then was joyful and straight.

You flourish now. The black earth swells
under the gentle touch of Bulgar hands.
The scent of wild geranium's on your breath,
your wind sings a new music.

Land like a human palm,
you're a universe to me.
I measure you not in acres
but in love, and I am drunk with you.

(W.M.)

Georgi Djagarov

ELEGY

Again there will be the scent of lilac,
tall beech-trees
again will be rustling
and the two of you—
you and my son,
will come here to seek me,
come here to find me, but
I shall be out of view.

I shall be a root
in the deep earth, spreading and sinking,
the welling sap that in strong boles shall rise,
I shall be a firefly
in the dark woods blinking
and a warm dew
on the lashes of your eyes.

(R. Wilbur)

Georgi Djagarov

SUMMER RAIN

Here it is so quiet
you can hear the twigs
whispering to each other.
Every leaf sags
under the heavy gold of the sun.
Such a wealth of gold
even the day stands still
holds it breath
to keep the gold from spilling
down into the weeds and underbrush.

(R.H.)

Georgi Djagarov

A CENTURY OF MIRACLES

Probably it will always escape them,
Those in the West, those rich men,
What it was our people fought to the death for
And would fight for again.

Or why bands of our brothers and uncles
Crossed fields and hills in those days before,
To build the Kremikovtzi plants,
To dig for coal and ore.

Those in the West who give orders, have they known
What it is to keen over this flung
Handful of black soil, Bulgaria?
Or if not to keen, to sing?

They come here weary and sated
And flash past in their sleek foreign machines
To tan their flesh at Sunny Beach
Or to bathe it in Melnik wines.

Let them do that. Good health to them.
The day will come when our work declares
They were not right, we were right;
The world is not theirs but ours.

And then their blear eyes will gaze up
At this century of bright miracles, knowing
The fiery rocket of our passage,
Seeing our hair blowing.

(W.M.)

Georgi Djagarov

NIGHT

Why aren't you sleeping, little one,
Why are you sobbing?
What is it that disturbs your dream?
The rustle of trees disrobing,
The far-off bell of a streetcar,
The fading voices of men,
Or the moon there rising
On the far-away hills again?
Or the owl that hoots in the woods,
Or a falling star
Stooping to perturb
The world's much-troubled rest?
Or is it my sleepless tossing
In wait for the coming day?
Why don't you slumber my little one?
Let sleep bear you away.

(W.M.)

Georgi Djagarov

WHY IS MAN BORN?

So the stones are dead, and the soil is mute,
And the sky is mute, the blank sky.

So the fire dies, and the leaves die,
And the stars at each daybreak die
In the blank sky.

So the wind blows and dies down,
And the water flows but flows down,
And songs fade away, and the voices of song are mute.

So tell me, then, of man who is soon to be stone,
Why is he born?

(R. Whittemore)

Georgi Djagarov

AFTER INTERROGATION

Two strides forward, two across.
The floor is slippery with ice.
Stretch your arms, you touch the walls.
Raise your head, you strike the ceiling.

And yet out there are boundless fields,
Deep rivers plunged.
The mountains echoing,
The sky
Flapped by its bird wings,
And rushing far away,
The roads.

There's your vast-expanding native land.
There are also the friends you've loved,
The dreams you've cherished,
And at least a space,
Just two strides wide,
Where you stand up
For all of these.

(T.W.)

AUTUMN

Farewell, said I,
If that's what you desire,
Be it so.
And the sea crashes away,
That black Black Sea.

Dearest,
We met here
By chance,
Like migrating sea-gulls.

And in the evenings
Stars,
A veritable host of stars,
Showered down on us.
But it's a fickle world.
Look! Our coupled footprints, broken
In the sand,
No longer linger there.

And as before
Our last words fade away
Unspoken.

Dropping its spell of yellow leaves,
It's the autumn,
The autumn,
That's claimed these lands.
I am trapped.
I am sentenced.
I know
I'll burn
At the stake of love.

Georgi Djagarov

The wind, blowing,
Drags broken brushwood by my feet.
Like a hangman
The horizon doffs its hood.
Someone's crying.
Why that crying?
It's no good crying.
In the deepening dusk I fade.

I burn.
Condemned to death,
Like the heretic
I vanish in smoke,
Like the skiff
In the turbulent gulf,
Like the shore in the dark.

I said farewell.
If that's what you desire,
So be it.
Farewell, farewell,
And the sea crashes away,
That black Black Sea.

(T.W.)

Luchesar Elenkov

"Me, 20-year-old sergeant, Ognyan, Mihailov,
the earth scrubbed from my greatcoat, the blood
washed from my face, my hair combed and parted,
my eyes flowering up from under autumn leaves.

Me, Ognyan Mihailov, risen from a trench of 1941.

My coat is filled with clouds of butterflies.
My face is tinted like old photographs.
My hair, stuffed in my cap, struggles out like wings.

And I, now almost sixty, after long absence
and agony in the trench, have come to greet you,
weary parents, old friends, who rest with me at dusk.

My work was bloody sweat upon the tongue
and the rattling out of last breaths. My work
was with bullets glinting like fish scales.
My work was with shells and jacketted slugs
and with the great hope
of staying alive, highpowered hope
in a gunpowder hell."

Yes, in 1941 this work could not be shrugged.

(J.B.)

Luchesar Elenkov

DEDICATION
(To Tamara)

Water splashes from the tap,
spills cold from the village fountain
where sunlight shimmers in copper jugs
that rock with the face of a poet.

Time stops for all this while
to pause about the chimneys.
We lived in Koprívshtitsa
bisected by a light.

Rooftops bring me back
to scenes almost forgotten.
I sense a powerful secret
that is to me forbidden.

Here will always be relived
what happened then between us.
I dip into a thought
that continues to disturb me:

the way you spoke with blood
ticking in your skin.
It is as if I lay
swirling at a vase's bottom.

Beside me, the edge of the field
is all aflame with flowers.
Behind me, I leave a spring
spilling from stony ledges.

(J.B.)

40

Luchesar Elenkov

PAINTER OF ICONS

Near dawn, still crouched on beechplank scaffolds
a man calls life up from the wet fresco.
From clay paint-pots, his brush talks with time
as our Lord and Satan stare at his moving hand.

Outside the church, in the snows of Preslav,
the eyes of howling wolves revolve about the moon
as the gray pack slinks off along the river bank
and red-capped roosters squawk upon a wall.

Snow and sunlight gather on the church eaves.
Inside, good and evil are drafting their designs.

(J.B.)

A LETTER TO
MY MOTHER IN VIDIN

Now autumn tints your orchard's leaves.
The cranes have flown full circle.
All afternoon, a cloud with reddish brow
hovers as if tethered to a tree.

And soon the links of autumn days
will drop to earth. The mountain's face
will stiffen ours in town, as ice
jams the brooks and rills fall silent.

And you will disappear with the summer
that's lost within this poet's heart.
Oh, someone surely will spread the word
that I am troubled and looking pale.

But only you can really tell
if river light has left my eyes
still dreaming of Vidin and boats
which brush along her river banks.

(J.B.)

Alexander Gerov

ON THEIR DAY OFF

The men relax within the bar,
a quiet smoky room
where nothing troubles them but beer.
They hum and talk and dream.

Their faces move in easy grins.
They dream and talk and hum,
all smiling as their glasses brim
in magic little suns.

(J.B.)

THE SUN

Our mothers are, at seventy,
already little girls,
waltzing under cherry blossoms
they cluck at peeping chicks.

The sun now smiles upon them
with tenderness and dread,
caressing them quite lovingly
and drops its blazing ax.

(J.B.)

THE TOWN TREE

Ah, Cosmos, are you conscious?
No. I'd say you aren't.
The starry night swoops down on me
so black and deep and large.

The tree has filled with ragged birds
that flocked and fell asleep.
They roost. Their tiny souls
screech terror through the tree.

(J.B.)

Vladimir Golev

TELL ME A LIE

Come on, lie to me.
Tell me you pine for me, need me,
That you've waited for me all these years,
Ever since you were a girl.

On stage you present
Truths, lies, treachery, deception—
So many human dramas
Come alive for you:
You can fall in love
And fall out of love,
Be somebody's plaything for a while
Without feeling,
Without coarsening.
Everything's beautiful.
The end itself is beautiful.

Come on, then lie to me.
To you, that's nothing.
Play Juliet to me in the failing light.
I'll be happy. I'll dream.
I'll try not to cry.

(W.M.)

46

Krassin Himmirsky

THE CRICKET

In vain we tried to banish him.
The roar of engines did not drive him away,
nor the asphalt with which we covered the fields.
We put up steel fences, walls of cement
                                and concrete.
Darkened the air with gas fumes
and shut ourselves in highrise buildings

But he, like a password
crossed every barrier unharmed.

And when we claimed victory
in the shade of a leaf, unseen
his fine string music started again.

Its tone reeled off our forgotten friends,
                        our forgotten homes,
                        our souls.
It recalled to mind
the world's forgotten beauty.

Then we looked for him,
meaning to speak in friendship at last,
but in vain.

He was nowhere visible.
And only within us
still rang and rang his refrain.

(D.L.)

Nikolai Hristozov

IN FRONT OF THE CAVE

The rain overtook us in the dusky wood,
throwing over us its long shadows.
At the mouth of a sudden cave
we found shelter—
I and you with the child.
We squatted under the grey vault
and you took the dripping child in your lap,
slowly loosened your hair
and wrapped him in it.

And there was the miracle,
familiar yet, ah, timeless to see.
That gesture, that wrapping in the cave!
When was it not, when will it ever not be?

(adapted W.M.)

INTROSPECTION

I breathe immortal air
and count my mortal days.
I see each sunset off
but the sun still burns inside me.
The winds pass overhead,
invisible they swarm,
but they sow seeds in my heart
of clouds and birds and trees.

Every breath of the world
sticks in my chest like a stone.
Battles call me to join them,
and issue me bleeding wounds.
After every defeat
I face the ranks defeated.

And the night comes down,
a strange lull floats in the air.

No, I did not expect,
did not want another fate.
This is century that called me
and gave me pride.

And now in my dream the second trumpet sounds,
sacrificial fires light my sleep.

Quiet I walk through the noisy babble of the world,
Spent bullets nuzzle my palms and burn out.
I cross to the far edge of the night,
my words sealed in kernels of silence.
I can feel them sinking invisibly
to where they came to me from,
to the ancient depths.
And when a verse spills on my page,
this is not a tear-stain, or a cry—
it is wounded silence.

(W.M.)

Nikolai Hristozov

OLD AGE

Now the day moves out,
flows with the wind's husk,
footsteps whisper their last
and melt in the dusk.

The sunset burns to embers,
on the hills gold dries to rust.
Green eyes glance in the west
and melt in the dusk.

Words, names fall away,
the earth fills with times past.
Next to a moon in the empty sky
there's a black cloud charged with lightning.

(W.M.)

Peter Karaangov

WINTER

A white street:
a white river.
Weather is always surprising.
You lift the curtain with your hand
and lo! beyond the window pane,
snow is falling.

And so it is
when between the two of you
a word is uttered
which causes pain.
In the room gone quiet,
surprised, you realize
snow is falling
between the two of you.

(adapted J.U.)

Boris Kristov

A BIBLICAL MOTIF

I live in the corner of the world where man,
with his head bent down over a plate,
is chewing fiercely. . . his Adam's apple
marking the passage of time.

Is this what I dreamt of when as a boy
I flourished a stick of spring onions amidst
whirls of dust, rolled the sun like an egg. . .
and went to sleep by it in a hole of darkness?

Why did merciless God choose me
to see the home-town thief
kiss the teacher's wife—to see their sweating
bodies steam that humid summer day?

When I crept out of a weed-covered childhood,
and my chin reached the boot of Goliath,
I realized that stupidity arching over me
like a ladle would keep me dry all my life.

Then I decided to join the poets,
to cool my burning head among them. . .
But a black sheep always lives apart from the flock,
Not wanting to be milked by the shepherd.

I saw them climbing towards the ridge of the mountain,
picking up stones for David's sling. David himself
was lying like a god in the river, hiding
his devil's tail from the eyes of all men.

(R.F.)

Boris Kristov

A WOMAN CALLED MARIA

With wild pears and a piece of bread in her bag,
She arrived. Throwing her shawl on my hands
She whispered: "My name is Maria. . .I am the woman
For all men, even those who are dead."

She turned my head like a top; she slipped in between
My sheets, and I fainted beside her perfect nipples.
Holding each other tight we split like ripe
Watermelons, until the old back of the sun cracked too.

But my candle burned in vain, and in vain
The warm milk trickled from the tea-kettle's eye.
She disappeared behind the white steam of a train,
The way a child runs into dust-clouds.

With wild pears and a piece of bread in her bag,
Perhaps she's now with someone else saying:
"Here I am. My name is Maria. . .I am the woman
For all men, even those who are dead."

But every wick burns out. She'll settle down, the wife
Of a jealous little gold-toothed man. She will hang
On his arm and drag him through life,
Keeping him tied with neckties and shackled in buckles.

And before she dies she'll go outside to shine
Her dusty shoes, preparing for death.
Then she'll fly, following geese to the clouds
Without even waving to the man at the threshold.

With wild pears and piece of bread in her bag,
She will reach heaven and shout
To the guard at the gate: "My name is Maria.
I am the woman for all men, even those who are dead."

(R.F.)

53

Boris Kristov

MY MOTHER'S WEDDING

He came down from the hills and vanished for ever,
My father: he sank amid the green grass in the field.
I've been waiting for him for twenty years now,
The twenty years mother has been always about to marry.
Men, well-dressed and carefully combed, keep coming.
They speak and implore, each offers his hand to her.
But her answer is "No." She says she's happy.
Then, she gets up and walks out of the house
To busy herself with something in the garden.
Later she returns with a pail full of milk,
And sits at the front door to have a talk with silence.
She's been like this as long as I remember.

But one day the man whom she'll marry will come.
The three of us will sit around the table.
Outside, clarinets will protest faintly, while
We will be silent, and our hearts will be silent.
She'll look at his hands fidgeting with crumbs on the table.
Afterward they'll start talking about their health.
Life will return to our poor little house.
Then, I'll bid them goodbye and leave.
My mother will weep at the threshold.
Late in the evening she'll go to sleep slowly,
Between the shoulder of the stranger
And the heart of my father dead.

(R.F.)

A PRAYER

The sleeves of fog's overcoat are dangling empty.
I put on the overcoat. It's exactly my size. I turn to
God who's driving his white chariot along the road,
and pray to him to remember all and everyone tonight:

"Give peace to the poor man, let him sleep till noon,
give money to the fool—let him fret when he spends it,
lift the dwarf up to the rim of a cask full of honey,
and let the actor get a part in the play;

invite the poet to dinner—make his pen a fountain,
and give oats to his horse (who's been living on verse),
sit for a while with the lonely man who's been waiting
so long, and to the gravely sick give (instead) pleasant little sneezes;

find a new, different, job for the hangman,
and squash the tick which drives women away,
fasten the belts of children travelling by air,
and lift up the old man who's struggling into bed;

provide the dead man with a warm cover and a good book,
make a paradise for the tree waiting at the corner. . .
and, please, help me God, to get back home,
so I may wash my mother's feet tonight."

(R.F.)

Nikolai Kuntchev

JELLYFISH

Jellyfish billow like galaxies
bobbing along the swells
to sting your ears
and scorch your sleepy eyes.

If it's true that we are here
just to paint a moral
aren't you slouched too low
beneath your crammed briefcase?

But you've read about the ocean too.
The jellyfish is the water's bell
tolling across the wave.
Beat it. School's out.

(J.B.)

HUNTING HORN

Oh, I shall never set out
to raise a gun against the lives
which make my images.

So when the shooting starts
bugler, blow loud, blow long, enchant
the hunters in their tracks.

Life is sweetest music
oh, much loftier and pure when
the horn in on the stag.

(J.B.)

Lyubomir Levchev

AGAIN

I watch the great clock
waiting for love.
On the minute hand
a dove has perched
lonely, like me.
Red clouds rise
in the silent afternoon.

The minute hand ticks
and falls a stroke lower.
The dove explodes
and flies away in terror
like an Egyptian soul.
Another wasted minute
hovers over the rooftops
and disappears.
Only the dove's fear
remains in my heart.

(adapted R.H.)

ROOFS

Grandfather's roof was made of slate .
and weeds grew on its craggy shelf.
"Where is my grandfather's house?" I ask.
"It fell in ruins all by itself,"

they tell me. "Look how we've paved the yard."
And there is the old roof, stone by stone,
flagging the court. But I can't believe
that that strong old house collapsed on its own.

It was a beautifully fashioned house,
cozy, in human kindness furled,
but alas it had the same defects
as Grandfather's vision of the world.

The thick slate roof was terribly heavy
and the house itself had no foundations.
Very slowly it sank in the ground
with fate of all such houses and nations.

I'm sure that old house didn't fall to pieces
but slowly, slowly, of its own great weight
sank till the roof is level with the earth
and now I walk like a cat on its slate.

Box-trees rise from the flues like smoke
while down below the hearth burns fair,
the pot is boiling—nothing is changed
in Grandfather's lost Atlantis there.

And father, a little boy, is curled
in Grandmother's lap. His eyes are wide.
"Quick, go to sleep now, the bogey man
is on the roof." Father listens, terrified.

Lyubomir Levchev

Yes! There is something there! He shudders
deliciously, and hearing proof
he falls asleep and dreams he dreams
my heavy footsteps on the roof.

It is cruelly hard to build a roof
that time's foundations can hold in place.
The superstructure (as Marx would say)
should never overload the base.

And those who write should think of things
as real as roof-trees, strong and straight.
Someone with lightning in his wings
has started walking on our slates.

(adapted W.M.)

P.S. INSTEAD OF A BEGINNING

They told me not to keep a diary
and to burn right away
whatever I wrote

I tried it
but I'm afraid I've burned
myself out.

America, wonderful and cruel,
you dissolve in the fire of my memory.
Finally you're more like a music.
The roads I've travelled
shine like dangerous strings
running along the fingerboard
of a strange guitar.
Towns flicker like mother-of-pearl buttons.
They would be difficult stops
for the devil himself to finger.

Who plays this infernal guitar?
Whose steely fingers dance there?
History, I feel your hand.
I don't ask you strum more softly—
I'm prepared to hear my roads broken
in discords of anger or reckless love.

And here I am, older now than the cypresses,
older than words, older than myself,
but still younger than the shot
that'll put an end to this diary.

(W.M.)

MY MOTHER IN PARADISE

The angels you're embroidering
in blue, the remaining blue of your eyes,
the gold little angels,
Mother,
the little angels
are waiting for you to finish
the last little wing.

And then,
they'll begin to sing,
fluttering around you.
They'll undo your hair
that sails out thin
and white,
and will lift you up to Heaven
like a Saint.

Your tortures will begin
in Paradise,
because in Paradise,
no one
looks like your son.

You'll bend your knees before the throne of God.
You'll wash His feet in tears,
entreating Him
to let you for a minute
return invisible
to our home. . .
to cook my breakfast,
brush my coat. . .
and write upon
my cigarette box:
"Do not be late tonight."

The Omnipotent will smile,
although He too is embroidered
in blue, the remaining blue of your eyes.
He'll say nothing in reply.

. . .You'll lie down alone
under the blissful palms.
You'll make a slit for a peephole
in a little secret star
of six diopters,
and look down on our neighborhood.

The sun will set in the windows
of our white apartment house.

Girls and boys in love
will stand like statues
in the shadows.
Women will be going by the shops
in their house slippers
calling their children
in lilting tones.

A winged boat will circle
over the airport.
Invisible trains
will whistle in the night. . .

Those train whistles
which are always taking me somewhere

You can hear them.
Listen to them!
Listen to them!
How they come
tearing a hole in the night. . .
How they cry at the level crossing. . .
One of them will be
crying for you.

(M.S.)

Lyubomir Levchev

BUREAUCRAT

Have I really ceased to exist
as a hope, as a man?
Have I turned into
some other kind of substance?

I watch myself reflected in the glass
that protects the polish of the table—
round table with no knights.
Although this is the hour for receptions
my only visitors
are vague anxieties.

I see myself floating among small clouds and pale ink,
and indeed, I am not true to life.
The white collar is the knife of a guillotine
No: an absurd directive addressed to nothingness.
My necktie gushes red from beneath my Adam's apple
it is warm and sticky.
My suit, official, is printed on paper.
The eyes are not my eyes.

There—the daily plane
is passing noiseless across the glass
that protects the polish of the table.
This time again it will
clear the heights of ashtray and card-file,
the vase of flowering pencils.
It will pass across my forehead.
It will turn into a paper plane
and land somewhere over there.

The hatch will open like a curse
and a confidential announcement
will descend the carbon-paper steps
to say that perhaps
I have really ceased to exist.

(W.M.)

BALLAD OF THE LADDER

The gallows swayed with laughter,
the hangmen laughed like children:
Climb up, climb up, comrade.
That's the ladder of freedom.

Her eyes duped by the glare,
her torn, scrabbling fingers
couldn't grasp the fact that the ladder
was painted on the wall.

She would attack its sheerness,
fall backwards to the ground,
get up and start again
as the whole world rocked with laughter.

O ladder of human suffering,
you would have broken to pieces
if you were made of steel,
if the wall were only stone.

But you are of stronger metal.
You're made from cruelty
You're painted on our walls
in the paints we bleed and weep.

Ah, suddenly the hangmen
are stunned, their humpback shadows
are frozen on the wall:
the woman has begun to climb!

The little, unknown woman
is climbing the painted ladder
that they had mocked her with,
that they had said was freedom.

Silent, majestic, peaceful,
the woman is climbing up
free as the blood-red moon.
Higher she climbs and higher,

Up the ladder to freedom.
Up the ladder to death.

(W.M.)

Lyubomir Nikolov

TWO PAINTERS

I: Van Gogh

Well, he lived among us and hated winters.
He moved to Arles where summer and bluejays
obliged him to cut off his ear.
Oh, they all said it was a whore
but Rachel was innocent. When cypresses
went for a walk in the prison yard
he went along and sketched them.
His suns surpassed God's.
He spelled out the Gospel for miners
and their potatoes stuck in his throat.
Yes, he was a priest in sackcloth, who hoped
that one day humans would learn to walk.
He willed mankind his shoes.

II: Picasso

He drank red wine and ate bread for lunch.
When he was really desperate, he created doves.
And because he suspected that no lands existed
he placed olive branches in their bills.
Yes, he was a lonely matador
in the Empty Arena. When wars drove in confusions
he greeted them with wandering painters
and ladies from Avignon.
He knew the Lord had hung the mountains out to dry
and would come one day to take them in.
He did not share this secret.
He was a shameless miser.

(*J.B.*)

Nino Nikolov

THE ROOM

What does one need?
A bed, and a table to work on.
And a telephone for connecting with people—
those one prefers to speak to from a distance.
For clothes, something loose and simple.
For a dictionary, whatever is latest.
And two or three chairs. Two is best,
because a third—I know from experience—
invites distraction.

(M.S.)

Nino Nikolov

THE CLOSET

What does a man leave
when he moves on,
the scent of cologne
or stale tobacco?
a piece of soap?
A dull razor blade perhaps
or the crumpled wrapping
from the new one he's taken along?
No. When he goes
a man leaves nothing
of any value to the newcomer.

(adapted R.H.)

Nino Nikolov

THE BEDROOM

Now finally, I have the time
to seek them out,
to guess their fortunes,
what side of the bed
he slept on, and if her hair
spread like light on
the morning pillow.
What did they bring and
what did they take with them?
Did a distant train whistle
keep them from sleep, the
noise of the street, the silence
of the room? Has a spider knit
that ceiling web since they've gone?
Did they use this waterglass?
Did they empty this winebottle together?
My friends speak to me in the
silence of this deserted bedroom.
There is no escaping the voices
calling from a blessed past.

(adapted R.H.)

Kolyo Sevov

A VISION

Sea spray glistens the marble god
as waves surge through its feet.
Salt mist traces the rigor of its face
as fog laves the statue and it darkens.
The god darkens with eternity.

At night, when waves roll with seaweed
and jellyfish open white umbrellas and
periwinkles poke from their shells, it is quiet.
So quiet one hears the footfalls of the dead.
This night, a sailor lies beached on the sand.

The tides have rocked him all his life.
His hopes have turned to salt.
The sea has stolen all from him.
The waves lick at his heels.
He is naked. He is nothing.

A god. Some seaweed. A corpse washed up.
The night crashes with madness.
The day was reefed on hopes.

(J.B.)

Kolyo Sevov

AN AFTERNOON'S
WANDERING

An empty ant track, scuffed by delicate feet.
The violent wind has passed. The hole gapes.
Corn will not sprout under lowering clouds.
The woodpecker's nailed to the bark of a tree.
No one can say what happened to the sky.

I fall to a dark place where words echo.
In the dunes in this well, sand sifts
through the clock of my cupped hands.
Is there any sense in measuring time?

When exposed by rains in an unknown future,
I'll be considered a significant find
as they measure my bones, skull span, and ribs.
No one will know my thoughts about myself.

(J.B.)

Kolyo Sevov

SONG BETWEEN
THE SEA AND SKY

For fifteen years I've sent words off on waves
to teach to you the secrets of the ocean bed
and you received them, along with echoes
from the beach and the fanatic flights of gulls,

viewing, unperturbed, both waves crashing ashore
—tamed and timid but keeping all my trusts—
and those that fell with furious pounding
on starlit nights when acacias dream.

Like sky and water we are merged
by perfect songs which rise and fall
to offer equally greeting and goodbye
in the nether zone that floats between us.

So if I should savor the daily flux of tides
and you should weary of being dashed
by sudden impulse, please do not sever
the rocking moon track leading us to shore.

(J.B.)

Kolyo Sevov

WHIRLPOOLS

My day went wrong: dark as a noose
twisted to wrench me, barren, from my root.
What harsh sky sent the motion? And you
who think tomorrow as you go,
wait till the whirlpools touch your feet,
between you and the shore, snatch you to rock
and fill your lips with sand and mud.
How else to cross the river?

Under water's blandest gaze, whirl-
pools wait. And I tell you this;
I would have gone airless, love, without a stroke,
had I not stared to you: a sun,
a blossom staring back, a lift of wings.

O easy to circle easy in my aimless ruin
had not my children like a blaze of angels
spun in my sky.
           My mother's body
thrust me into a light in which birds
measured out distance to the sea, and wind
cried through the autumn bones of fathers.
It was no time of nurture or of music,
but, winter mother, that cold dirt
fostered the seed.

(J.J.)

Liliana Stefanova

THE UGLY MAN

I touched his scar, but
only with my eyes.
The scar. It marked him.

Face stamped with sorrow.
eyes without spark:
he had no hope of kindling
responsive fire in me.
                        Indeed,
he avoided looking
at me looking at him.
He was ugly.

I didn't want
to win someone just because
he was weak, pitiful—ugly.
I didn't want a prize
I'd not had to strive for.

But suddenly ugliness
demanded its rights,
presented its credentials:
impressively clean shirt,
upright posture,
confident walk.

Everything in me that wanted
to turn tail turned back,
turned into galloping cavalry.

I forgot that he was ugly. Discovered

his high forehead, thick lashes, the racing
of quiet original thoughts.
I saw deep in his eyes.
Handsome!
         A handsome man.
How could I not have noticed
his strong fingers scattering
seeds of desire?

All at once
the world was more beautiful.
Lead me onward,
ugly beauty!

(adapted D.L.)

Liliana Stefanova

I SEE AGAIN

Evening swallows the gulls,
the chalk of their wings,
the dire cobalt of the sea,
in a moment, perhaps, me.
I tell it, welcome—
you give me back
what has been taken from me.

Summer glare has crazed my eyes.
Like a feather-brained driver
blazing undimmed oncoming lights,
it has blinded me.
My irradiated mind
no longer quarrels
either with lies or with truth—
to that dead organ
enlightened and benighted are the same.

Now the firm handwriting of dusk
joins in a cursive script
all differences—
earth with sky,
rapture with sulky offense,
love with guilt.
Rhythms become legible
which I could not read
in the giddy blaze of day.
What dimensions we lose
to vainglory and spectacle.

And how vainly seek in that dazzle
true image, true response.
It is an enviable faculty of the soul
to see in twilight
beyond distance and for once clearly.

(adapted W.M.)

Liliana Stefanova

AND THE SUMMER
STILL PERSISTS

You hold in your embrace
much of the sun.
The hot sunlight of July
has given your skin
its brown. This southern colour.
And the summer still goes on
—no late autumn,
no chill wind,
no whisper of
sick leaves falling.

And summer still persists.
I relax
in the tremor of your solar ring
and blend
with your image of July,
and everything, now past, returns:
the sand,
the boat,
the scorching heat.

I don't know
if it's to the sun or you
I say quietly:
Don't go. Keep me warm.
I'm yours.

(*adapted W.M.*)

Stefan Tsanev

STRANGE BIRD

Something terrible happened.
Some kind of bird
settled down under the eaves
of the house next door.
It might have been a swallow or a sparrow—
nobody paid attention at first,
and afterwards
it did not matter.

The bird brought straws, feathers and petals
to build its nest,
singing enthusiastically.
Nobody paid attention at first,
and afterwards
it did not matter.

One morning the bird brought a piece
of string or thread,
and tied one end to the nest.
Nobody paid attention to it at first
and afterwards
(until ten o'clock)
it did not matter.

At ten somehow
the bird hanged itself:
though its wings resisted a long time
though the neighbors looked long
expecting something to happen
or someone to do something,
the bird went on dying,
bravely, quietly, dying.

Who made the noose?
Who made the noose?
It's strange that nobody paid attention to this
at first, which afterwards
became a terrible matter.

Husbands kept pregnant wives
away from the windows,
mothers kept children in the kitchens,
old women started looking for their Bibles
lost somewhere among the other books,
or slipped away under their beds.

And the hanged bird swayed in the wind
like the pendulum of a clock,
as we became aware of time, its passing.

I can't get out of my mind the thought
that if birds
have started hanging themselves,
something is wrong on this earth.

(R.F.)

Stefan Tsanev

HAMLET XX

Soliloquy of a museum figure in
Hiroshima, which stands for humans
lost in the atomic blast.

The earth is billions of years old.
They say its weight is growing
because of objects falling from the skies.
They say its movement's slowing down,
and that the moon too is slowly falling towards it.
A new glacial period is coming, is what they say.
I am not surprised.

Nature offers examples of astounding metaphors:
near Hiroshima birds flew underground,
displacing earth with their wings instead of air,
fish left the ocean
and perched in tree-branches,
sea-turtles lost the ancient
sense of direction,
and, desperate, plunged into the desert's waves.

These are terrible things to us,
but to the great earth they are nothing,
it goes on rotating, it goes on
        circling round the sun—the sun, too,
        rotates and circles round,
        moving and circling spheres. . .

But the sun is a provincial star
in a provincial galaxy.
The earth is a green electron
somewhere in a little finger
of the galaxy.
And we humans are the same.

We, too, are galaxies.
We, too, have our satellites.
We, too, have fingers,
fingers deft at drawing the knife,
fingers deft upon the trigger.

(R.F.)

Ivan Tsanev

TREE ON THE HILL

I should not forget
the tree upon the hill
out there, somewhere,
wherever: a tree with no name
familiar with the falling night.

A tree on a hill
summoning up bright moments
when I meandered through the weeds
and calling up the hollows of the dark
where crickets trill.

A tree on the hill.
Let it remember and desire me.
And since it has no name, I'll call it
Patience or Green Silence.
A tree, a graceful bending
of my thought
stretched out into the sky
and tossing with the clouds.

(J.B.)

Nikola Vaptsarov

SONG

Over the forest
over Pirin
the wind howls
thin.

We set out, seven of us
to fight.
Far above, Pirin stayed behind
in its starry night.

With creatures of the woods
we hid by day.
This is how by night
we made our way:

By the look of the grass
we understood
where the rain had rinsed
our fathers' blood

By reading fallen leaves
we found
our mothers' places
underground.

And from rust-colored soil
we guessed
where our first loves
lay down to rest.

Seven set out
on that attack.
Seven of us.
Three came back.

(W.M.)

EPOCH

Machines, steel, machines
and oil and steam and stink.
In the sky, concrete chimneys.
In the hovels, ghostly hunger.
In Mexico the golden corn is burned
in steam boilers to keep it dear
and slaves with cracked lips
harvest it night and day.
Elevators roar, the engine shakes its fist
in time's old face.
Man has broken gravity's spell
and today flies
faster than the free bird.
But still life weighs on us,
shackles our wings mercilessly
with tough rope,
chokes us on the poison mould
of old rust.
The surge of our lives is pressed down
by the steel helmet sky.
And, below, the people's dark sea
swirls turbulently.
Vain slogans of brotherhood—
life builds a wall.
Life, the inveterate spender
replies cynically—war! war!
And what about the countless starving?
War! What about the purposeless death?
And what about our wellspring of youth
which shakes the world?
An epoch of savage cruelty
galloping insanely forward.
Epoch of molten steel
on the brink of a new world.

(W.M.)

86

BIOGRAPHICAL NOTES

Elisaveta Bagriana (b. 1893) is one of the foremost poets of Bulgaria. *Everlasting and Holy* (1927) marked the beginning of her career. Her later works, including *From Shore to Shore* (1963) among many others, show a broadening of her themes and a concern for political and feminist issues.

Miriana Basheva (b. 1947) graduated from Sofia University in English literature. Her first book of poetry, *Bad Character*, set the tone of her later writing, hard-edged and often experimental. She has done translations from Russian and English as well as play and film scripts.

Georgi Belev (b. 1945) has a degree in mechanical engineering. At present, he works for the *Literary Front* weekly, the central literary tabloid in Sofia. He is the author of *A Deciphered Inscription* and *Moderately Cloudy*.

Georgi Borisov (b. 1950) graduated from the Gorky Institute in Moscow. His two books of poetry are *At Noon Somewhere in the Beginning* and *Let Him Be*. He is deputy editor-in-chief for *Fakel*, a magazine of contemporary Soviet literature.

Bozhidar Bozhilov (b. 1923) graduated from the Sofia University Law Faculty and is the author of more than thirty books of poetry. He has also written novels, plays, essays, and has translated from English, Russian, and German poetry. He is director of the Narodna Kultura Publishing House.

Atanas Dalchev (1904-1978) was born in Salonika and studied philosophy and pedagogy in Sofia. With his clear images, with his famous *Fragments* (1967), and with his translations from the French, he remains an important modernist voice in Bulgaria.

Blaga Dimitrova (b. 1922) is the author of nine books of poetry, four novels, and three plays. After studying Slavic literatures at the University of Sofia, she did postgraduate work at the Gorky Institute in Moscow. In the United States her poems have appeared in *Ms.* magazine, in *The New England Review*, and in *The Poetry Miscellany*.

Georgi Djagarov (b. 1925) was born in Byala village, fought as a partisan in his teens, was imprisoned by the Germans, and later studied at the Gorky Institute in Moscow. Besides his several books of poetry, he is the author of a celebrated play, *The Prosecutor* . He is Vice-President of the State Council of Bulgaria.

Luchesar Elenkov (b. 1936) is from the Danube area that he frequently writes about. He is the author of several books of poetry and is currently General Secretary of the Union of Bulgarian Writers.

Alexander Gerov (b. 1936) is a writer of science fiction as well as poetry. He has served as director of literature programs for Radio Sofia. His many books include *The Very Best* (1970) and *Short Fantastic Novels* (1966).

Vladimir Golev (b. 1922) was born in Bansko in the Pirin mountains and studied law at the University of Sofia. He is the author of twelve books of poetry and editor-in-chief *Septemvri*, the most authoritative journal for contemporary Bulgarian literature.

Krassin Himmirsky (b. 1945), the former Bulgarian Cultural Attaché in Washington, is the author of a recent book, *I Do Believe*.

Nikolai Hristozov (b. 1931) was a young activist in the anti-fascist movement and later studied literature at the University of Sofia. He is a translator of Pablo Neruda's *One Hundred Sonnets on Love* and the author of several books of essays as well as nine books of poetry, including the recent *Snow in the Nest*.

Peter Karaangov (b. 1931) is from Sandanski and has been a librarian, a journalist, a playwright, and a film editor. He is editor-in-chief of *Plamuk*. Among his more recent books are *Sudden Summer* (1970), *Coming Snows* (1971), and *The Rain before Turning into Snow* (1976).

Boris Kristov (b. 1945) showed his particular flair for metaphor in his first book of poetry. He participated in the International Writers Forum in Iowa and is known as well for his experimental fiction.

Nikolai Kuntchev (b. 1937) has translated widely from French and Russian, including a volume of Leonidze's poetry. In his own poetry, particularly *A Presence* (1965) and *Wondrous Things* (1973), he is known for his bold use of language.

Lyubomir Levchev (b. 1935) comes from Troyan. President of the Union of Bulgarian Writers, he is also one of the most highly regarded of contemporary poets, with many of his poems in the explosive style of Mayakovsky and Yevtushenko. He is the Vice-President of the Committee for Culture and a member of the Central Committee of the Bulgarian Communist Party. Among his thirteen books of poetry, some of the most popular are *Recital* (1968), *Observatory* (1967), *Starway* (1973), and *Freedom* (1975).

Lyubomir Nikolov (b. 1954) recently participated in the International Writers Forum at the University of Iowa. His first book is *Called by the Tides*.

Nino Nikolov (b. 1933) is known for his essays on literature and his numerous translations from Hungarian and Russian as well as his own poetry. His most recent books are *Every Homecoming Is Silent* and *Reflections of a Distant Shore*. He has studied at the University of Iowa as a guest in its International Writers Forum.

Kolyo Sevov (b. 1933) is Secretary of the Writers Union on the Black Sea at Varna and himself has spent many years in the Bulgarian merchant marine. He is editor-in-chief of *Prostori*, a literary quarterly. His interest in the ancient, Thracian past of Bulgaria often comes up in his poetry. Among his many books of poetry, essays, scripts, and interviews with foreign writers are *Autumn Sea, Oncoming Winds*, and *A Pledge*.

Liliana Stefanova (b. 1929) comes from a family of antifascist activists. She is the author of *Magnetic Field*, a book of poetry, of *Japan without Kimono and Fan*, a documentary, and *A Fall in America*, a record of her visit to the United States and Mexico. She is President of Bulgarian PEN.

Stefan Tsanev (b. 1936) studied journalism in Sofia and dramaturgy at the Moscow Film Institute. At present he is playwright and artistic director for the Theatre Sofia. Among his better known titles are *Hours* (1960), *Chronicles* (1965), *I Ask* (1975), and *Saturday '23*, a play.

Ivan Tsanev (b. 1941) graduated from Sofia University in Russian literature. He writes poetry both for adults and children and works for *Plamuk*, a magazine of contemporary literature. Among his books are *A Week* (1968), *Sunday Earthquake* (1973), and *Telegram* (1977).

Nikola Vaptsarov (1909-1942) was born in the Pirin mountains and became a ships engineer and mechanic after attending the nautical school in Varna. He was an early member of the Communist Party and spent most of his life as a professional revolutionary. He was shot by a firing squad in 1942. In his poetry, he shows a determined love for common people and common things. He became known as a poet when his *Motor Songs* was published in 1940.

NOTES ON TRANSLATORS

John Balaban is the author of two books of poetry, *After Our War* and *Blue Mountain* as well as a recent novel, *Coming Down Again* (Harcourt Brace Jovanovich, 1985).

Roland Flint's most recent book is *Resuming Green: Selected Poems, 1965-82* (Dial Press, 1983). He is Professor of English at Georgetown University.

Richard Harteis is Director of the PEN Syndicated Fiction Project and author of *Morocco Journal* and *Fourteen Women*, books of poetry from Carnegie-Mellon University Press.

Josephine Jacobsen is the author of *The Chinese Insomniacs* (University of Pennsylvania Press, 1981) and *A Walk with Raschid & Other Stories* (Jackpine Press, 1978). She has served as Consultant in Poetry to the Library of Congress.

Maxine Kumin's most recent book of poetry is *Our Ground Time Here Will Be Brief* (Viking, 1982), which includes new and selected works. A former Consultant in Poetry to the Library of Congress, she was awarded the Pulitzer Prize in 1973.

Denise Levertov's works include *Candles in Babylon* and *Light Up the Cave* (New Directions, 1982). She has received the Morton Dauwen Zabel Prize for poetry, a Guggenheim Fellowship, and a grant from the National Institute of Arts and Letters.

William Meredith is a former Consultant in Poetry to the Library of Congress and a Chancellor of the Academy of American Poets. His most recent book of poetry is *The Cheer* (Alfred A. Knopf, Inc., 1980).

May Swenson is the author of *New & Selected Things Taking Place* (Atlantic-Little, Brown, 1978). With Leif Sjöberg, she is translator of *Windows & Stones: Selected Poems* by Tomas Transtromer (University of Pittsburgh Press, 1972). She is a Chancellor of the Academy of American Poets.

John Updike's most recent novel is *The Witches of Eastwick* (Alfred A. Knopf, Inc., 1984). Along with Balaban, Flint, Harteis, Kumin, Levertov, and Meredith, he has visited Bulgaria as a guest of the Union of Bulgarian Writers. His recent book of poetry is entitled *Facing Nature* (Alfred A. Knopf, Inc. 1985).

Theodore Weiss's latest book of poetry, *A Slow Fuse: New Poems*, was published by Macmillan Publishing Co. in 1984.

Daniel Weissbort's new book of poetry, *The Lease Holder*, is published by Carcanet Press in England. He is Director of the MFA Translation Program at the University of Iowa.

Reed Whittemore is the author of eleven books, including a celebrated biography of William Carlos Williams. His most recent book of poetry is *The Feel of Rock: Poems of Three Decades* (Dryad Press, 1982).

Richard Wilbur's latest book of poetry, *Opposites: Poems and Drawings*, was published by Harcourt Brace Jovanovich in 1979. He has recently translated Molière's *Four Comedies* and Racine's *Andromache*, both published in 1982 by Harcourt Brace Jovanovich. He has won the Pulitzer Prize, the National Book Award, a Guggenheim Fellowship, the Edna St. Vincent Millay Award, the Prix de Rome, and a Ford Fellowship.

FOREST BOOKS

Special Collection

THE NAKED MACHINE Selected poems of Matthías Johannessen. Translated from the *Icelandic* by Marshall Brement. (Forest/ Almenna Bokáfélagid)
0 948259 44 2 cloth £7.95   0 948259 43 4 paper £5.95   96 pages

ON THE CUTTING EDGE Selected poems of Justo Jorge Padrón. Translated from the *Spanish* by Louis Bourne.
0 948259 42 6 paper £7.95   176 pages

ROOM WITHOUT WALLS Selected poems of Bo Carpelan. Translated from the *Swedish* by Ann Borne .
0 948259 08 6 paper £6.95   144 pages. Illustrated

CALL YOURSELF ALIVE? The love poems of Nina Cassian. Translated from the *Romanian* by Andrea Deletant and Brenda Walker. Introduction by Fleur Adcock.
0 948259 38 8 paper £5.95.   96 pages. Illustrated

RUNNING TO THE SHROUDS Six sea stories of Konstantin Stanyukovich. Translated from the *Russian* by Neil Parsons.
0 948259 04 3 paper £5.95   112 pages. Illustrated.

East European Series

FOOTPRINTS OF THE WIND Selected poems of Mateya Matevski. Translated from the *Macedonian* by Ewald Osers. Introduction by Robin Skelton.
0 948259 41 8 paper £6.95   96 pages. Illustrated

ARIADNE'S THREAD An anthology of contemporary Polish Women poets. Translated from the *Polish* by Susan Bassnett and Piotr Kuhiwczak.
0 948259 45 0 paper £6.95   96 pages.

POETS OF BULGARIA An anthology of contemporary Bulgarian poets. Edited by William Meredith. Introduction by Alan Brownjohn.
0 948259 39 6 paper £6.95   112 pages.

THE ROAD TO FREEDOM Poems by Geo Milev. Translated from the *Bulgarian* by Ewald Osers. UNESCO collection of representative works.
0 948259 40 X paper £6.95   96 pages. Illustrated.

STOLEN FIRE Selected poems by Lyubomir Levchev.
Translated from the *Bulgarian* by Ewald Osers.
Introduction by John Balaban.
UNESCO collection of representative works.
0 948259 04 3 paper £5.95   112 pages. Illustrated.

AN ANTHOLOGY OF CONTEMPORARY ROMANIAN POETRY
Translated by Andrea Deletant and Brenda Walker.
0 9509487 4 8 paper £5.00   112 pages.

GATES OF THE MOMENT Selected poems of Ion Stoica.
Translated from the *Romanian* by Brenda Walker and
Andrea Deletant. Dual text with cassette.
0 9509487 0 5 paper £5.00   126 pages   Cassette £3.50 plus VAT

SILENT VOICES An anthology of contemporary Romanian women
poets. Translated by Andrea Deletant and Brenda Walker.
0 948259 03 5 paper £6.95   172 pages.

EXILE ON A PEPPERCORN Selected poems of Mircea Dinescu.
Translated from the *Romanian* by Andrea Deletant and
Brenda Walker.
0 948259 00 0 paper £5.95.   96 pages. Illustrated.

LET'S TALK ABOUT THE WEATHER Selected poems of Marin Sorescu.
Translated from the *Romanian* by Andrea Deletant and
Brenda Walker.
0 9509487 8 0 paper £5.95   96 pages.

THE THIRST OF THE SALT MOUNTAIN Three plays by Marin Sorescu
(Jonah, The Verger, and the Matrix).
Translated from the *Romanian* by Andrea Deletant and
Brenda Walker.
0 9509487 5 6 paper £6.95   124 pages. Illustrated

VLAD DRACULA THE IMPALER A play by Marin Sorescu.
Translated from the *Romanian* by Dennis Deletant.
0 948259 07 8 paper £6.95   112 pages. Illustrated.

Fun Series

JOUSTS OF APHRODITE Erotic poems collected from the Greek
Anthology Book V.
Translated from the *Greek* into modern English by Michael Kelly.
0 948259 05 1 cloth £6.95   0 94825 34 5 paper £4.95   96 pages.